MONEYMAKERS

by Ingrid Roper
illustrated by Susan Synarski

PLEASANT COMPANY PUBLICATIONS™

Good Cents for Girls

Published by Pleasant Company Publications
©1998 by Pleasant Company

Printed in the United States of America.
98 99 00 01 02 WCR 10 9 8 7 6 5 4 3 2 1

American Girl Library® is a registered trademark of Pleasant Company.

Editorial Development: Michelle Watkins, Julie Williams
Art Direction: Kym Abrams
Managing Art Director: Marilyn Dawson
Design: Andrea Burke

Library of Congress Cataloging-in-Publication Data
Roper, Ingrid, 1970-
Moneymakers: good cents for girls / by Ingrid Roper ; illustrated by
Susan Synarski.
p. cm.
Summary: Presents ideas, tips, and true accounts to encourage girls to
make, manage, and save money. Includes business starter tools such as
business cards and price tags.
ISBN 1-56247-668-8
1. Money-making projects for children—Juvenile literature.
2. Entrepreneurship—Juvenile literature. [1. Moneymaking projects.
2. Entrepreneurship.] I. Synarski, Susan, ill. II. Title.
HF5392.R66 1998   98-21076
658' .041—dc21   CIP   AC

Dear American Girl,

Have you ever wanted to make money of your own? Then add a new buzzword to your vocabulary: entrepreneur (ahn-treh-preh-NURR). It means someone who starts and manages a business.

What does it take to be a good entrepreneur?
- Imagination to see what people need
- Creativity to come up with an idea that fills that need
- Spirit and spunk to get to work
- Determination to finish what you start
- Courage to believe in yourself when others tell you an idea won't succeed

To begin, decide what you're good at, what you love, and what you have fun doing. Do you love animals or little kids? Try a dog-walking service or run a children's story hour. Like to get organized and keep things tidy? Try a silver-polishing service or offer to straighten people's cupboards. These are the skills you can put to work in a business of your own.

After all, the real secret to earning money is to do something well, love what you do, and have the courage to do it. Moneymakers is full of ideas, advice, and tools to help you on your way.

Good luck!

Pleasant T. Rowland

Pleasant T. Rowland
American Girl Entrepreneur

Contents

Cute as a BUTTON

10 "Cents-ible" Tips

Start making **"cents"** with these **10** basic steps.

1. Choose a Moneymaker

Make a list of what people want or are too busy to do. These are their needs. Then make another list of all the things you enjoy and do well. Compare the lists. Can you match a need with a talent or skill? If you like to make crafts, and family or friends often need unique gifts to give, you've found a moneymaking opportunity!

what I Like
crafts
animals
rollerblading

what People Need
help with recycling
unique gifts
babysitting

2. Time Yourself

How much time do you have? Choose a moneymaker that fits your schedule. If you are starting soccer season or starring in the school play, you probably shouldn't agree to babysit every afternoon. If you take a job, make sure it stays *your* job. Sure, everyone needs help sometimes. But if your mom or dad regularly ends up doing your paper route, it won't be fair to any of you.

3. Get the Word Out

Begin with the people you know and trust. Show friends your handmade jewelry or ask a neighbor if she wants her garden weeded. Don't be afraid to speak up. Even people who don't hire you may pass your name on to a friend. Hang flyers, signs, or banners, and pass out business cards to let people know what you do. You can also place ads in neighborhood newsletters or your school newspaper, but ask your mom or dad first.

7

4. Start Smart

Figure out how much money you'll need to start your business. Write down all the supplies and materials, and list their prices. Can you borrow this money from a parent or family member and pay it back with the money you make later? Or can you earn it doing an odd job? Be sure to write down a goal of how much money you want to earn with your money-maker. Your goal will change over time, but it will help you get started. Determine whether you'll need extra space, too. If you plan to make a craft corner in the basement, ask first.

5. Set a Fair Price

Your price should be fair to you and your customer. When setting prices for things you make, first add up the costs of all your materials. You can cut some costs by buying supplies in discount stores. You want to be able to pay for those costs and earn a little more for yourself—that's called *profit*. But don't charge more than what people are willing to pay. Compare your prices to what other products like yours cost. If you are trying to set an hourly rate for a service, find out what other kids your age charge for similar work.

6. Study Up

Whatever your moneymaker, you may want to learn more about it before you hang an "Open for Business" sign. Take a babysitting class. Read craft books. Interview experts to find out their secrets to success. Then get plenty of practice. Spend time with the toddler next door while an adult is around. Test your lemonade recipe on family or friends. Perfect the bows on your gift wrapping. The better you become, the more successful you'll be as a moneymaker.

7. Set the Terms

Before doing any work, talk with your customer about exactly what you will do and how much you will charge. Then put it in writing. If a customer offers to pay you less than you think you should earn, don't just back down. Talk about why you want to charge more. Maybe there's a middle price that will be fair to both of you.

8. Be of Service

Be on time, be professional, and work hard. Treat your customers with the kindness and care you would give to a teacher, relative, or friend. Greet them with a smile and be sure to thank them for their business. Always try to do more than your customers expect. Help kids with their homework while you babysit, or stack newspapers in a neat pile for vacationers. They will be impressed and will not only want to give you more work but may recommend you to others.

9. Stay Safe

Always let your parents know where you are and how to reach you when you're working. Never sell door-to-door alone. If you're selling with friends in a public place, it's perfectly all right to talk with strangers who are buying things from you. But if anyone ever makes you uncomfortable, get away from him or her and tell an adult immediately. Trust your instincts.

11

10. Add It Up

Measure how successful your moneymaker is by keeping records of how much money you make and spend. If you earn more than $400 in one year, you may need to pay taxes to the government. Talk to your parents about what, if anything, you owe. Being a successful money-maker also means managing your money well. You deserve to spend a little money, but plan on putting some back into your business for supplies or advertising. Save the rest for something special!

True Story

Rachel puts her **love** for **pets** to work by walking dogs.

Rachel Lilley

Entrepreneur, age 13

Business: Dog walking
Location: California

Start-Up

I needed a way to earn money to buy things for my own dog, Sadie, and I wanted to do something I liked.

Money Made

$225. Summer is the best because I have more time and can walk dogs more often. What I charge depends on the dog and the owner. I make $5 a day for walking a Scottie twice a day, and $2 for walking a Yorkie once a day.

Worst Business Day

One day I looked away for just a second and Heidi, a lab-dachshund mix, lunged after a cat. I chased them all over the yard. Now I always keep a good hold on the leash!

Best Business Day

I walked six dogs after school. Then I went home and walked my own!

Secret to Success

I do a good job. Customers trust me with their keys and their pets. It's important to be responsible and to give the dog a really good workout.

Rachel's Advice

Customers will trust you if you have a good reputation. Do what you say you will. Really listen to what the owner tells you. Find out what kinds of tricks or commands the owner wants the dog to learn, and give the owner weekly updates. I have taught a puppy to sit and a dog to twirl on its hind legs!

Dog Days

Make **money** and have doggone **fun** watching, washing, and walking pups.

Spotless Pups

Ever notice how dogs love to shake and splash in water? Whether you scrub the pup indoors or out, your dog wash guarantee is a squeaky-clean pet and no messy puddles. Be sure to clean up after the wash and to hang towels out to dry. For a finishing touch, tie a crisp red bow around the dog's neck.

Dog Wash Today

SHAM

Wagging Walkers

Walking dogs is a great way to play outside with girl's best friend. Get instructions from the owner about how long to walk the dog and what behaviors to watch out for. Be responsible, on time, and careful with keys, and don't forget to bring a baggie for doggie messes. Most of all, have fun. Your job is to wear the playful pooch out and to return the dog calm and happy. You can earn more money walking a couple of dogs at a time, but only if the owners agree to it.

June 2

Snickerdoodle couldn't wait to get to the park today. He didn't even stop to sniff Mr. Parker's roses.

Dog Log

Keep owners up-to-date with a pet log when you pet-sit. Decorate the cover of a spiral notebook with the pet's name and picture. Each day that you visit, record and draw pictures of what you and the pet did. Write a report on new tricks or old habits. Then leave the log for the owner to read.

GOOD CENTS

Get the Word Out

Dog lover will deliver attention and love at least three times a day. References available. Call Carrie 555-0942

Pass out eye-catching flyers in your neighborhood offering to walk or watch animals while owners are away. Also offer *references*, names and numbers of satisfied customers who will recommend your service. Be sure to ask for their permission first.

Critter Sitter

Take charge by asking owners these important questions before you **pet-sit.**

Playtime

What does your pet like to do? Does she have a favorite toy? Where does she like to be petted or scratched?

Basic Care

Does she need to be groomed? When and where does she go to the bathroom? How often should I clean up after her?

Mealtime

When should I feed her? How much should I feed her? Can I give her treats? Is she allergic to anything?

Training Time

Should I use any special commands or sounds to get her attention? What good or bad habits should I watch out for? How should I praise her? How should I scold her? Where isn't she allowed to go?

GOOD CENTS

Check It Out

Keep a checklist to make sure the owner always returns to a pampered pet and a neat home.

- ☐ check and replenish water and food.
- ☐ Make sure pet isn't pawing, pecking, or chewing furniture, clothes or shoes.
- ☐ Clean up any messes.
- ☐ write a log entry about any special activities or behavior.
- ☐ Stack mail or newspapers in one place.
- ☐ Lock up when you leave.

Pet Presents

Sell **personalized,** playful gifts for the family pet at craft fairs and yard sales.

Bowl 'Em Over

Take orders for one-of-a-kind pet dishes and leashes. Write pet names in bright letters with markers or paint on plastic pet bowls. Add playful touches like mice for a cat bowl or bones for a dog bowl. Use fabric puff pens to personalize leashes and collars with squiggles, flowers, or dots.

The Right Price

How do you know what price to charge? First, add up the cost of materials. Then find out what others charge for a similar service or product. To compete, you may have to offer a better price or product. And don't forget that your time counts. Charge enough to "pay" yourself for time and money spent and to make a profit.

True Story

Fair prices and the **right location** are the keys to Molly's success.

Molly Goebler
Entrepreneur, age 12

Business: **Refreshment stand**
Location: **California**

Start-Up

I didn't have the money to buy something, so I borrowed it from my little brother. My parents got mad. They said, "Wouldn't you feel better if you made that money for yourself?" So I made some brownies and lemonade, and I set up a table outside my house. I got the money I needed. It was so much fun, I did it every week that summer.

Money Made

$150. I like it that people can get a snack and a drink for 50¢. I make yummy desserts, and a lot of people like them.

Worst Business Day

I was 10 feet down our driveway instead of right up on the curb. Kids were drawing at the table and it looked like we were just playing. I made only $3 that day.

Best Business Day

One of our neighbors had a garage sale, and they asked if I would like to sell at their sale. Almost everyone bought something. I made $35 in one day!

Secret to Success

I sell brownies, lemon squares, cookies, and glasses of lemonade for 25¢ each. Some people say 25¢ is a steal, but I think I sell more because it's such a bargain.

Molly's Advice

Set up your stand in a spot that's close to your house. It's good to have a school, park, or library nearby. Put up bright, colorful signs with an arrow pointing toward your stand. To find garage sales where you can set up a stand, look for ads in the paper, and keep your eye out for sale signs in the neighborhood. Then ask if you can sell at the sale.

New & Improved

Make bestselling snacks by adding a new twist to old favorites.

Cupcakes in a Cone

These ice cream cone cupcakes are easy to make and eat. Prepare cake batter as directed on box. Place ice cream cones in a muffin tin, and fill cones one-fourth full with cake batter. Bake and cool. To frost, dip and swirl the top of each cupcake cone in a bowl of frosting.

Top with colorful confetti sprinkles. Wrap and sell at bake sales or a snack stand. Take orders for birthday parties, holiday parties, and club meetings.

Chocolate Dunk

Sell chocolate-covered pretzels for a sweet and salty snack. With an adult's help, place chocolate chips in a bowl and microwave on medium-high for 1 minute, then stir. Continue microwaving for 30-second periods, stirring in between, until smooth. Use tongs to dip pretzels in chocolate. Place on cookie sheet lined with wax paper. Decorate with sprinkles. Freeze to harden, then bundle in colorful plastic wrap.

Pop and Top

This tongue-tingling cheesy-ranch popcorn is guaranteed to wake up tired taste buds. Pop 12 cups of popcorn. Melt 2 tablespoons of butter, and combine with popcorn in a large plastic bag. Sprinkle 1 tablespoon of dried ranch-style dressing mix and 2 tablespoons of cheese-flavored topping over popcorn. Close bag tightly and shake to coat evenly. Package individual servings in small brown lunch bags or in plastic baggies.

GOOD CENTS

Before You Bake

Prepare to bake by asking yourself these questions: Is my snack or drink easy to make and sell? Do I have enough time? What do I need to buy? How much do the ingredients cost? Read carefully through recipes and gather all ingredients and utensils before starting.

Bundle of Yum

Attract customers with **pretty** packaging that is **easy** to do, and cheap, too!

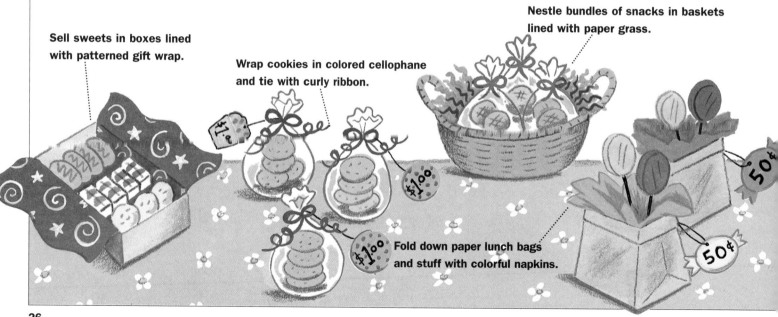

Nestle bundles of snacks in baskets lined with paper grass.

Sell sweets in boxes lined with patterned gift wrap.

Wrap cookies in colored cellophane and tie with curly ribbon.

Fold down paper lunch bags and stuff with colorful napkins.

GOOD CENTS

Kitchen Care

- Ask about and follow all house rules in the kitchen.
- Work with sleeves rolled up, hair pulled back, and apron strings tied.
- Wash hands, tools, and cooking surfaces before and after handling food. Wipe up spills right away.
- Dry hands before plugging in appliances. Turn off appliances after you're finished.
- Ask an adult to help you with the oven or microwave and when using knives. Use oven mitts or pot holders to handle hot items.

Decorate straws with construction paper cutouts shaped like suns, lemons, or bananas.

Make fun labels and price tags by decorating construction paper with rubber stamps, glitter, or stickers.

Out-Standing!

Try these secrets to a successful **refreshment stand.**

Tasty Treats

Whether you wheel your sweets around in a wagon or set up a tempting table of snacks, giving customers tasty treats is the key to a super snack shop. Before you set up shop in a public place, find out if your city or community requires a license.

Post signs. Make sure prices are clear to customers.

BAKE SALE

drinks 50¢
popcorn 50¢
cookies $1⁰⁰

Keep your stand neat and clean. Always have a trash can nearby.

Dress up your table with a colorful tablecloth and fresh flowers.

Give away free samples. Offer a variety of foods and flavors to appeal to different tastes.

Bring plenty of coins to make change.

FREE SAMPLES ↓

Offer napkins to scoop up spills and wipe off hands.

Mind the temperature. Use coolers and ice to keep cold items cold and thermoses to keep hot items hot.

Hit the Spot

Set up shop at the **right location** and sell nifty nibbles to satisfy cravings.

On the Path

Sell trail mix to hikers and bikers.

On the Sidelines

Beat the heat at soccer or baseball games with chilled lemonade.

At the Stadium

Brew hot apple cider to warm fans' hearts at tailgate parties.

By the Pool
Sell fruit juice to thirsty swimmers at pool parties and swim meets.

At the Theater
Satisfy sweet tooths with home-made candies during intermission at a community play or concert.

In the Park
Set up a Popsicle pit stop at a popular Rollerblading spot.

Box It Up!

Create **cookie care packages** that customers can send to family and friends.

Made with Care

Neighbors with kids at camp or college won't be able to resist buying your cookie care packages. Sell homemade cookies to friends, family, and teachers, too, who may want to treat a friend who's under the weather. Offer to fill packages with different varieties, and charge by the dozen. Wrap the cookies up tightly and cushion with unbuttered popcorn so they make it safely to their final destination. Deliver with care to customers and include a bill for the amount due.

True Story

Annie earns money **babysitting, helping** at parties, and **tutoring** kids.

Annie Cubera

Entrepreneur, age 12

Business: **Babysitter, party helper, tutor**

Location: **Michigan**

Start-Up

I wanted a lot of things and I needed a way to earn money. I really like kids, so I handed out flyers to my neighbors offering to babysit, help kids with schoolwork, or help moms with their kids' birthday parties. I got more clients than I ever expected. Now it feels great to buy things myself instead of asking my parents for money.

Money Made

$300. I made $5 an hour tutoring a girl in reading. When I babysit I make $2 an hour. But I made more money tutoring because I brought books and word games to teach her new words.

Worst Business Day

One time I was playing in the snow with a two-year-old boy. I threw a snowball at him, and he started to cry. He snapped out of it when I showed him a huge icicle. But I learned that even though I play with little kids as if I'm their age, I'm older and stronger and need to be careful.

Best Business Day

I led games at a birthday party. The kids I babysit were excited and proud of me. They wanted me to meet all their friends and to show them how I do a cartwheel. We all had a great time. And the mom was happy because she could talk to her relatives at the party.

Secret to Success

I enjoy what the kids enjoy and really focus on them. I'm good at guessing exactly what game, activity, book, or song will work for the kids on a certain day. And parents call me again because they know their kids have fun with me.

Annie's Advice

When you're with kids, plan lots of things to do. Always clean up games, art supplies, and toys after you're finished with them. This is easier than doing all the cleaning at the end, and it keeps the mom happy because her house isn't a disaster.

Beyond Babysitting

Boost your babysitting clout with these **out-of-the-ordinary** kid-care ideas.

Homework Helper

Hold a weekly study session for kids who need extra help in a subject you are good at. Ask teachers and friends to help you spread the word. Use flash cards to build vocabulary and math skills. Organize a mini spelling bee. Start a "read-aloud" book club. Be sure to give kids and parents positive feedback.

Buddy System

Make money walking children to and from school or the bus stop. Introduce yourself and your service to parents you see taking their kids to school, or ask the crossing guard or bus driver to suggest new customers. Sing songs and play word games as you walk with your new buddies. Just remember to be on time and to obey traffic signals and crossing-guard rules.

Once Upon a Time

Host a story hour each week at your house. Pass out flyers at the local library and around the neighborhood listing the book of the week. Charge a few dollars for each kid and ask parents to make *reservations,* or to let you know in advance who will be coming.

GOOD 🪙 CENTS

Study Up

Jump-start your babysitting career by taking a babysitting class at your local YMCA or Red Cross chapter. You'll learn important first-aid and safety tips. Then gain hands-on experience by being a mother's helper. And become a pro by joining a club and sharing ideas with other babysitters.

Tot Watch

Whether at home or away, parents often need an **extra** set of **hands** to keep children at play.

Birthday Helper

Start a children's birthday party business. Offer to blow up balloons, decorate, serve refreshments, and plan and lead games. Prevent party squabbles by keeping guests busy and entertained. Play games in which everyone wins and each child gets a turn. And don't forget to help clean up after the party!

Kids Only

Set up a sitter shop at backyard barbecues, community meetings, and even yard sales. Make a "kids-only" area, register children with a sign-in sheet, and give each child a name tag. Make masks, paint faces, or tell stories. Watch the community paper for moneymaking events.

Cover Your Bases

Watch tots during baseball games or other sports events so parents can keep their eyes on the ball. Organize your own peewee Wiffle ball game or play Follow the Leader.

GOOD CENTS

Super Service

Before taking charge, put parents at ease by asking these questions:

- How long will you be gone?
- Is there a number where you can be reached?
- Whom should I contact in case of an emergency?
- Are there any safety reminders?
- Are there any rules I should be aware of?

Sitter Season

Earn money hosting holiday fun for **little ones.**

Bunny Business

Play the bunny at Easter egg hunts. Put the word out about your bunny business to friends and parents in the neighborhood. Buy colorful plastic eggs and fill them with candy, trinkets, or pennies. Hide the eggs in clever places like behind a flowerpot, in a mailbox, at the bottom of a drainpipe, or in a doghouse. Then hop away and let the fun begin.

Ghouls' Guide

Take kids trick-or-treating in your neighborhood. Before leaving, get the rules about how much candy kids can eat and when they need to be home. Follow safety rules when crossing streets, remind kids to walk—not run, carry a flashlight, and always say "trick or treat" and "thanks." Set a good example by being the first to wear your jacket if it's cold or raining.

Holiday Craft Shop

Invite parents to drop their kids off at your holiday craft shop on their way to the mall. While parents get their Christmas shopping done, you can help kids make crafts for their own holiday gifts. Choose inexpensive, simple crafts such as sweet-smelling sachets or evergreen wreaths. Charge parents for your time and materials.

First-Night Watch

You'll be at the top of every parent's sitter list when you host a kids' party on New Year's Eve—the most popular babysitting night of the year. Make glittery party hats, serve sparkling grape juice, and let the kids make as much noise as they want at the stroke of midnight.

Pro Pointers

Even **pros** know it's **important** to keep these babysitting basics in mind.

Arrive on time.

Family Favorite

The secret to becoming a family's number one babysitter is to have fun with the kids while keeping them busy and safe. Plan plenty of activities. Find out what the kids like and want to do. Share new ideas and crafts with them, too.

Wear clean and comfy clothes.

Keep important numbers and safety tips handy in a babysitting notebook.

Pack new games and puzzles.

BABY SITTER LOG

True Story

Claire's **computer know-how** and **customer care** keep her in the money.

Entrepreneur, age 13

Business: Graphic designer
Location: Texas

Start-Up

A friend at school showed me her father's business card. I told her that I could make her one with my new computer. I brought her card in the next day, and soon every girl in my class wanted one.

Money Made

$400. I pay for all my paper, and I'm lucky that my parents let me use the computer. Once I made a book about a friend's trip to Africa, and I used two ink cartridges in two weeks. That time I asked the customer to pay me for supplies.

Worst Business Day

A girl in my class asked if she could buy a card for Mother's Day. I told her I would give it to her the next day for $1. Another girl said she'd make it for free. I didn't know what to do. As a friend, should I offer to do it for free, too? But if I did, would everyone want me to design for free? I didn't make the card, and sometimes I feel sorry about it. The worst part is the other girl never made the card either, so our friend didn't have anything for her mom.

Best Business Day

When I got orders my first day, I suddenly saw what I could do, and it felt incredible! Now I take orders for hundreds of cards, but those first orders were the most special.

Secret to Success

I'm not afraid of the computer. Sometimes people get angry and call it names. But I don't get emotional. I just try to solve the problem and get the program to work.

Claire's Advice

Always give yourself enough time on a job to do your best. It's important to show your best customers that you appreciate their orders. I give gift certificates or discounts to people who order from me again and again.

Desktop Pro

You'll be in demand when you can **type,** **design,** and **publish** on command.

Word Tech

Are you a fast, accurate typist? Start a typing service. Post flyers at school and around the neighborhood offering to type homework, reports, and letters. Charge by the number of words or pages typed.

News Hound

Do you want to organize a neighborhood cleanup or keep club members in the know? Create a newsletter on your computer. Sell copies, subscriptions, and even advertisements.

Poochie Pals
Call Susie

Allison's
Baby Care
555-0987

Dana's Design Co.

Flyers
Banners
Letterhead
Logos
Business Cards

Reasonable Prices!
Quick Turnaround!
Call 555-0102

Cookie Care
Saturday Delivery
Call Julie 555-1112

February

Jr. Designer

Do you have an eye for type and layout? Open up your own design agency. Create signs and banners for birthday parties, bake sales, or community meetings. Design personalized calendars using scanned photos or artwork. Typeset stationery and print on fancy paper. You could even design logos and business cards for other moneymakers!

47

Useful Bits

Do a top-notch job meeting customers' needs and giving super service.

Meeting of Minds

Before you start a big computer job, set up a meeting with your customer to talk about what he or she needs and how you can meet those needs. At the meeting, agree on pricing, brainstorm ideas, and set a *deadline,* or a date when you will have the work finished.

Perfect Work

To be sure your computer project is perfect, run a spell check before printing it out. Remember that even a spelling checker doesn't catch all errors, so proofread your work carefully by reading through the copy and making sure all changes were typed in correctly. Your attention to detail will give customers confidence in you!

Finish Line

When you finish a project, arrange to meet with the customer again to review your work and get feedback. Deliver the finished project with a bill that tells exactly what work was completed and how much the customer owes you.

Pay Day

A Girl & Her Computer
1234 First Street
Anytown, USA
555-5544

June 4
To: John Jacobs
1238 First Street
Anytown, USA

Description	Total
1 banner	$2.50
6 Flyers	$3.00
100 price tags	$5.00
Total Due	$10.50

Please Pay on Delivery

Thank You!

Don't be shy—ask customers to pay you when you deliver a project or finish a job. If a customer is unable to pay on the spot, send out a bill every two or three weeks as a reminder of how much is owed.

49

Great Greetings

Create greeting **cards** on your **computer.** Sell a bundle for birthdays, holidays, or any **special day!**

YOU WILL NEED

- **8½-by-11-inch card stock**
- **Word processing, paint, or drawing program**
- **Blank envelopes**

1 Using guides, divide an 11-by-8½-inch page into 4 equal squares. Type a message or insert an image in the center of the bottom right square. This will be the front of the card.

2 Type your name, the name of your business, and your business logo in the bottom left square so customers will be able to call and reorder. Print page on card stock.

3 Fold printed card stock from top to bottom, then side to side. The message or image should appear on the front of the card, and your logo should appear on the back.

Fancy Fringe

Use colored paper and trim edge of card with pinking shears.

Lace It Up!

Punch holes around border of card and lace with a ribbon or shoelace.

Sell Smart

Set to Sell

Sell bundles of six cards with blank envelopes.

Surprise!

Make and sell confetti to stuff in your cards.

Carry samples of your designs in a portfolio or in a folder in your backpack. Show them to friends, family, neighbors, or anyone who may be interested in ordering cards, flyers, letterhead, banners, or other designs. Keep order forms handy!

Wired Ways

Make money **sharing** your computer **smarts** with others.

INTERNET CLASS
SAT MAY 18th

Computer Tutor

Organize training sessions for families or friends who have just purchased a new computer or who are learning new software. Introduce beginners to the Internet by searching for a favorite sport or hobby. Teach kids how to draw with the mouse and play computer games. You can also start a computer hot line that customers can call for help. Charge for the time you spend helping them. Hand out business cards and flyers with your phone number and hours of availability, but check with your mom or dad first.

GOOD CENTS

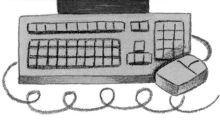

Stay Safe

- Ask your parents for permission before posting your name or e-mail address on the Internet.
- Don't answer e-mail that makes you feel uncomfortable.
- Never arrange to meet face-to-face with someone that you've met online unless you talk it over with your parents first and have an adult present.

True Story

Rosalind and Katie team up to get the job done in half the time.

Katherine Swick
Entrepreneur, age 10

Business: **Odd jobs**
Location: **Connecticut**

Rosalind "Lindy" Baldwin
Entrepreneur, age 14

Start-Up

Katie: My mom wanted me to make some money of my own and to learn how to save. She helped me brainstorm ideas for jobs. I decided it would be more fun with a friend, so I asked Rosalind to work with me.

Money Made

Rosalind: $70 each. We make flyers on Katie's computer and list lots of jobs we can do. We give the flyers to people in the neighborhood. Our prices depend on the job and how hard it is. We split the work and the money in half.

Worst Business Day

Rosalind: On one of the hottest days of summer, a neighbor called us to dig rocks out of her garden. Rocks were everywhere. After three hours she paid us $2 each. We told her we usually make more than that, but she said she didn't think it was very hard work. We should have set a price before doing the work.

Best Business Day

Katie: We got two calls in one day! One job was to walk two really cute dogs named Buttons and Max, and the other was to pick raspberries.

Secret to Success

Rosalind: We don't just do a job fast to get it done. We do a really good job, and we do it in half the time that it would normally take because we work together.

Katie's Advice

Always do the same amount of work. Don't fight over money. Make sure everything is equal. It's okay to laugh. It makes the work go faster, but don't get too silly or people won't think you're working very hard.

Rosalind's Advice

It's okay if you're good at different things. I'm taller than Katie, so when we pulled down ivy from someone's fence, I pulled the high vines while she worked on the lower ones. The important thing is that we work well together.

Chum Fun

Is the job too big for one? **Double up** with a friend for twice the fun.

Lawn Lovers

If you have a green thumb or are handy with yard tools, start a lawn-and-garden service. Water lawns, dig and weed flower beds, trim hedges, winterize gardens, and rake and bag leaves. Always leave the yard or garden neat and tidy. Put tools back, sweep up dirt, and compost clippings.

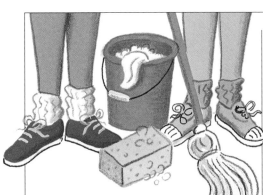

Bucket Brigade

Attack dusty, disorganized garages and basements using brooms, brushes, sponges, rags, and mops. Clean from top to bottom. Offer to organize the space. Sort old clothes and books for donation. Separate nails, screws, and other hardware and put in glass jars. You can even offer to help organize a garage sale.

Winter Wonders

Go door-to-door with a friend and offer to shovel snow from sidewalks and driveways. Teamwork will get the job done quickly so neighbors can soon be safely on their way. Keep a standing order with customers to shovel snow after every snowfall. But if you say you'll do it, make sure you do.

GOOD 🪙 CENTS

Set the Terms

Yard Girls PRICE LIST
Weeding ....$ɯ
Raking/bagging Leaves .... =ɯ
Lawn/garden watering .....$ɯ
Snow Shoveling .....ɯɯ

Doing odd jobs often means charging different prices based on the amount and type of work you do. Write out or type up a price list to let customers know exactly what you expect to be paid.

Incredible Sale!

When you and your friends need to make extra money, clean out your closets and have a yard sale.

Stockpile Stuff

Find out what you have that you can sell. Gather old sports equipment, clothes, furniture, tapes, CDs, toys, dolls, and games. Ask your mom or dad before you sell anything.

Get Organized

Meet with your friends to set a date, time, and place. Pick a weekend day for your sale and choose a busy location. Get permission from a parent or neighbor whose yard you want to use.

Shout About It

Tell everyone you know—friends, neighbors, and relatives. Make signs and flyers and hang them in your neighborhood. Place a small ad in your community paper.

AN INCREDIBLE SALE!

when? This Saturday, July 25
8 a.m. to 3 p.m.

where? 1726 Elm Street

what? Huge selection of clothes, books, toys, music and games.

Shine and Polish

A week before the sale, meet with friends to spruce up your goods. Set fair prices and mark them on colored stickers. Code each girl's things with a different color so you will know how much each girl sells. Plan to bring tables and chairs to display your items. Assign shifts for refreshment, cashier, and sales jobs. Start saving coins so you can make change at the sale.

Ready and Waiting

On the day of the sale, set up at least an hour early. Arrange tables and chairs. Group similar items together and display everything with style. Use a cigar box or an old jewelry box for a cash register. Keep track of earnings by putting the colored stickers from sold items into envelopes labeled with each girl's name. Have bags, extra stickers, pens, and a calculator on hand.

Sale Away

To keep customers browsing longer, sell brownies, cookies, and lemonade. When the last customer leaves, count your money, add up the prices from each girl's envelope of stickers, and give each girl the money she made. Everyone should pitch in to clean up. Donate leftover items to a local charity.

Party Pals

Make money by **helping** out at festive feasts and parties. Let the hosts entertain guests while you and a few friends look after the **details.**

Before the Party

- Decorate the party room.
- Polish silver.
- Set the table.
- Arrange flowers in vases.
- Answer last-minute calls from guests who need directions.

At the Party

- Take coats at the door.
- Serve finger food and drinks. Don't forget the napkins!
- Keep snack bowls full.
- Keep the music playing.
- Collect and wash empty glasses and plates.
- Make sure the family pet doesn't escape from the basement or bound out any open door.
- Smile and spread cheer!

After the Party

- Put leftovers away.
- Load the dishwasher.
- Take out the trash.
- Before you leave, ask if there is anything else you can do, then present a bill to the host for the hours you and your friends worked.

Teamwork Tips

It's important to be professional when working with a friend. But don't forget your friendship is priceless. Here are some ways to keep things fair:

- Do the same amount of work.

- Swap jobs so no one gets bored.

- Treat each other with respect. Sometimes one of you might need to be the boss, but that doesn't mean you should be bossy.

- Split earnings equally.

Clean Up!

Get a group of friends together to **raise cash** with a super-organized **car wash.**

Squeaky-Clean

Organize an assembly-line car-and-bicycle wash. Split up the work into different jobs. Have one friend greet customers and take money, one vacuum, one wet and rinse, one soap and scrub, one dry and polish, and one clean windows. Set up chairs and spread newspapers and magazines on small tables so customers can relax while they wait. If it's a hot day, wear bathing suits so you can keep cool while working.

True Story

Diana's crafty **bookmarks, bookplates,** and **pencils** are all the rage at school.

Diana Leigh Smarrito

Entrepreneur, age 14

Business: Rainbow Library
Location: New Jersey

Start-Up

My friends and I were always trading books, so I decided it would be fun to have a library. I put Rainbow Library cards inside my books and lent them out to friends. They liked my library so much I started making and selling bookmarks, bookplates, and pencils to go with the books.

Money Made

Almost $200. I made a lot more money my second year because I told more people about my products and because buying things from Rainbow Library became a fad in school.

Worst Business Day

At first I spent a half hour making reading packs with bookmarks, pencils, and book-plates. I sold each pack for 15¢. My friends bought everything, and one of them said she couldn't believe it was so cheap. When I saw how little I earned, I realized I wasn't charging enough for my time.

Best Business Day

When I raised my prices, I was nervous no one would buy anything. But it all sold that day!

Secret to Success

I pass out a list of everything I have for sale and keep a few ready-made products in my locker so customers don't have to wait for their orders. I also add new products and designs all the time to keep customers interested.

Diana's Advice

Write down how long it takes you to make things and how much you spend on supplies. Don't price things too inexpensively. Keep track of what everyone orders so you know what they have. Then when you add new products, you'll know what those customers like and what to show them. I have a notebook with all my orders and a list of who has what.

Made-to-Order

Customers won't be able to resist special-ordering these **one-of-a-kind** crafts!

Autograph Pencil

Personalize pencils with clever letters and playful prints. Rub a piece of sandpaper over the painted part of a pencil. Then paint over the sanded area with acrylic paint. Let dry. Use a paint pen to write a name on the side of the pencil. Then add fun designs like squiggles, flowers, stars, and hearts.

I.D. Barrettes

Paint a metal barrette with bright nail polish. Let dry. Use a paint pen to print the customer's first name on the front of the barrette. Add doodles and fun patterns. Let dry. Then tie a piece of embroidery floss onto the end of the barrette and string letter beads to spell out the customer's last name.

Taking Orders

Keep these tips in mind to deliver perfect products every time:

Last Detail

Review all colors, styles, sizes, and shapes with the customer.

Spell Check

Are you adding initials or names? Ask for the correct spelling, write it down, and check it with the customer.

Special Delivery

Agree on how, when, and where you'll deliver the finished product. Ask for the customer's phone number. Call if you finish early or have questions about the order.

Bead-Dazzle

String ABC beads to create **personalized** pendants, key chains, and friendship bracelets.

YOU WILL NEED

- An adult to help you
- Fimo or Sculpey clay, two colors
- Wooden skewers
- Toothpicks
- Baking tray
- Oven mitt
- Satin cord or embroidery floss

1 Roll and shape pieces of Fimo or Sculpey clay into beads. Carve letters into the beads using the tip of a wooden skewer or a toothpick.

2 Roll a different color of clay into small, thin strips. Use strips to fill in the carved letters on the beads.

3 Stick a skewer through beads, wiggling beads to widen hole for stringing. Place on baking tray. Ask an adult to help you bake beads, following directions on package.

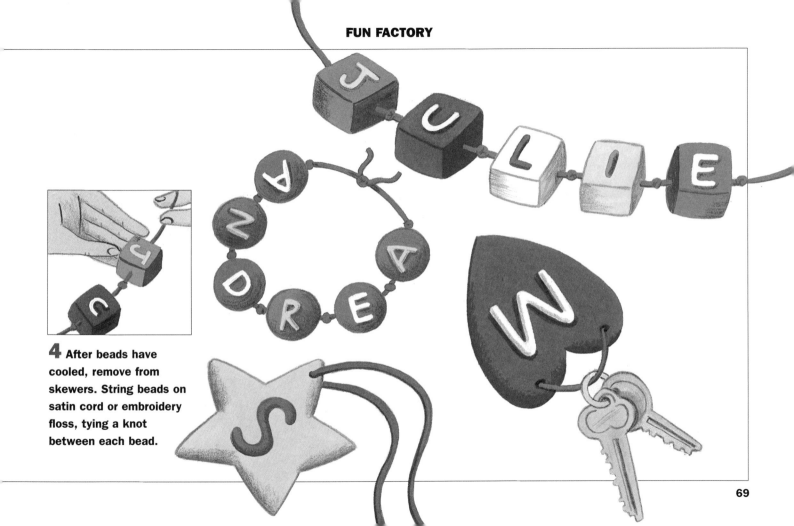

4 After beads have cooled, remove from skewers. String beads on satin cord or embroidery floss, tying a knot between each bead.

Seed Money

Put your **green thumb** to work growing, packaging, and selling seedlings.

Garden Starters

In late March or in April, fill peat pots half full with potting soil. Sprinkle three flower or vegetable seeds in each pot. Cover seeds with soil, and use rubber bands to secure plastic wrap around pots. Place in a sunny window. Water seeds frequently, keeping soil moist. When seedlings are 1½ inches tall, remove plastic and pull out all but the biggest plant from each pot. Leave pots in the sun and continue watering. By May, seedlings will be ready to package and sell!

Plant Stand

Set up a booth to sell seedlings at farmer's markets, yard sales, and spring festivals.

Offer to plant the seedlings you sell.

Green Thumb cares for Gardens too!

call KELLY 555-GROW

Sell herb seedlings such as basil, dill, mint, and oregano in brightly painted clay pots.

GREEN THUMB Seedlings $1.50 each

Grow and sell catnip for cat lovers, or edible flowers for gourmet cooks.

Pillow Pals

Create a craze with cute **key-chain charms** and **zipper pulls.**

YOU WILL NEED

- Felt or polar fleece
- Pencil
- Ruler
- Scissors
- Straight pins
- Ribbon, 3 inches long
- Needle
- Embroidery floss
- Polyester stuffing
- Lanyard clips or
  key rings
- Paint pen, googly
  eyes, buttons, or pom-
  poms for decoration

1 Fold fabric in half. Trace a 3-by-3-inch shape for pillow. Cut out both layers and pin together. Loop ribbon, and pin between cutouts at top of shape.

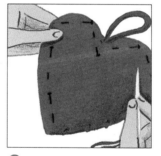

2 Thread needle and knot end of thread. Starting at the bottom, *whipstitch* pieces together by sticking needle through the back of cutouts and pulling through the front.

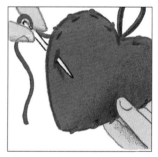

3 Bring needle around to back. Begin another stitch ¼ inch from first stitch. Continue sewing until you have a 1-inch hole left. Be sure to stitch through the loop.

Sign Here

Sell autograph pillow pals. Friends can sign them with a fabric or puff pen.

Button Up

Sew on buttons, charms, or patches to make one-of-a-kind pillow pals.

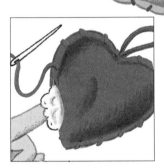

4 Set threaded needle safely aside. Stuff polyester fill through hole. When pillow is full, stitch hole closed. Knot thread and remove needle. Attach clip or key ring to loop.

Zoo Pals

Create animal faces with embroidery floss, pom-poms, and googly eyes.

Show & Tell

Advertise your pillow pals by clipping samples onto your backpack or key chain. Soon you'll be answering questions and filling orders!

73

Cute as a Button

Recycle **buttons** into playful **bracelets** and fancy **frames.**

Fun Photo Frames

Paint plain wooden or cardboard frames in bright colors. Let dry. Glue buttons of different shapes, sizes, and colors onto the frames. Frame pictures cut out of magazines and display at craft fairs or yard sales.

Frames
$3.50

Button Bracelets

Cut a 12-inch-long piece of elastic cord. Loop cord through holes in a button and tie knot. String buttons of different shapes, sizes, and colors onto cord. When you've strung 6 inches of buttons, knot cord. To finish, thread leftover cord through holes in the first button and tie knot.

True Story

Annie stays **organized** and always keeps her **goal** in sight.

Annie Harrigan

Entrepreneur, age 12

Businesses: **Veggie stand, car wash, and stationery design**

Location: **Kansas**

Start-Up

I wanted to buy a radio. It took me a long time to work and save for it, but I finally got it. I save my money in a yellow hatbox. Whenever I have more than $100, I take it to the bank.

Money Made

$350 since I started five years ago. I made $150 last summer at a vegetable stand selling fresh tomatoes, corn, lettuce, and carrots from my garden. My friend and I also held six weeklong car washes.

Worst Business Day

We had our first car wash for just a day and no one came. The next time we scheduled it for the whole week and put up flyers with directions, times, prices, and fun slogans.

Best Business Day

Once my friend and I started a canned-food drive for a food bank and gave free stationery to everyone who donated. We helped feed hungry people and also got a lot of orders from customers who liked our stationery and wanted to buy more.

Secret to Success

Each year I set a savings goal. I post the amount on my bulletin board. Having the goal in sight makes it easier to save and to not spend money on things I don't need.

Annie's Advice

Be organized. I carry order slips and samples of stationery around with me. At home I keep samples of stationery in one box and cards that I'm ready to deliver in another box. I also write down in a notebook everything I spend for supplies.

Setting Up Shop

The secret to success is staying organized. Clear some space and create a **mini office** to call your own.

Desk Set

Stock up on office supplies like pens, a calculator, a stapler, an address book, a telephone book, paper, envelopes, paper clips, folders, and stamps.

Time on Your Side

Keep a clock in sight or wear a watch to track time while working.

It's a Date

Carry an appointment book or planner with you wherever you go. Record important school, work, and play dates. Keep a "to do" list to look over and update each day.

File Away

Keep important business papers such as bills, receipts, and letters at your fingertips. Sort papers by subject and file them in folders. Then put the folders in alphabetical order and store them in a desk drawer, filing cabinet, or box.

Girl at Work

Hang a sign on the door of your office or on the back of your desk chair to let brothers, sisters, or parents know when you are hard at work.

Check-In

Schedule a weekly update with your mom or dad to talk about what you will be doing in the next week and to look over your ledger or savings book.

Super Promotions

Spread the word about your moneymaker with **business cards, doorknob flyers,** and **price tags.**

Smart Cards

A business card is like a small ad that promotes your business. Make your own cards and hand them out to customers so they will know what you do and how to contact you.

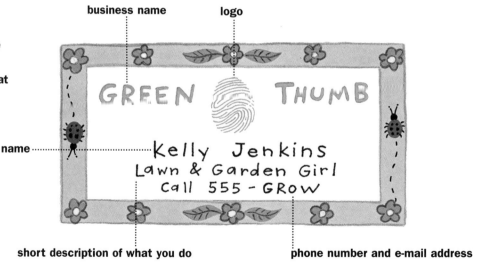

business name

logo

name

GREEN THUMB

Kelly Jenkins
Lawn & Garden Girl
Call 555 - GROW

short description of what you do

phone number and e-mail address

Door-to-Door

Get noticed with flyers that you can hang on doorknobs. Design, cut out, and distribute in your neighborhood.

Terrific Tags

Set your business apart from the competition with eye-catching price tags and labels. Cut cute shapes out of construction paper and decorate with glitter, ribbon, stickers, and your logo.

Picture Your Business

Create a *logo*, or symbol, to use on your business cards, stationery, labels, and flyers. A logo can either contain the name of your business or be a picture of something that represents, or stands for, your business. Play with different styles of type or draw a picture to capture the spirit of your moneymaker.

Paper Trail

Find actual business **forms** you can **use** at the back of this book!

Order Form

If you sell or make something that can be ordered ahead of time, fill out an order form with the customer to make sure you deliver a perfect product. Write down the quantity, color, price, special instructions, delivery date or time, and customer info. Give the customer a copy to keep. Then get to work filling that order!

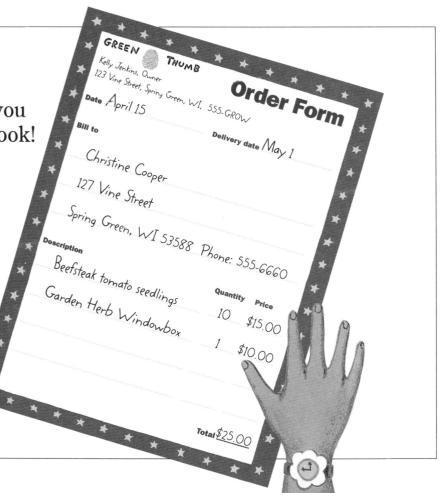

GREEN THUMB

Kelly Jenkins, Owner
123 Vine Street, Spring Green, WI, 555-GROW

Order Form

Date April 15

Bill to

Delivery date May 1

Christine Cooper

127 Vine Street

Spring Green, WI 53588 Phone: 555-6660

Description

Beefsteak tomato seedlings

Garden Herb Windowbox

Quantity   Price

10   $15.00

1   $10.00

Total $25.00

Bill

Write up and deliver a bill to show what work you did and what the customer owes you for it. Give the customer a date to pay by. Keep a copy of the bill for your own records. When the customer pays you, mark your copy "Paid."

GREEN THUMB
Kelly Jenkins, Owner
123 Vine Street, Spring Green, WI 53588, 555-GROW

Bill

Date May 3

To Anne Hamilton

Black Dog Ranch

Spring Green, WI 53588

Description **Price**

April 21: 2 hours weeding @ $3.00 per hour $6.00

May 1: 1 hour planting @ $3.00 per hour $3.00

Please pay by 5/15

Thank You!

Total $9.00

Receipt

When a customer pays you cash, offer to provide a receipt describing what was bought and how much was paid.

GREEN THUMB

Receipt

Date May 1

1 basil seedling $1.50

2 tomato seedlings $3.00

Total $4.50

Customer Care

Make a file to keep **important** customer **information** at your fingertips.

Customer File

Write customer names, addresses, and phone numbers, plus any special notes, on index cards. Keep the cards in alphabetical order in a shoe box or a drawer. When you need to drum up business during summer break or find out who to show new products, you'll know who to call.

Hamilton, Anne

Address: Black Dog Ranch
          Spring Green, WI
Phone: 555-7007
Rate: Gardening $3.00/hr., seedlings $1.50
Special Notes: Garden needs weeding once every two weeks.
          Planted tomato seedlings May 1.

TOMATO seeds

Babysitter File

If you're a babysitter, you'll want to write down even more information about your customers, including emergency numbers and favorite games.

Meadows, Chelsea
Birth Date:

Breen, Jack

Birth Date: 5/18/93
Parents' Names: Lisa & Patrick
Address: 1127 Ruhlman Avenue
Phone: 555-8008
Rate: $4.00/hr.
Emergency #:   Mrs. Goldie Williams (grandmother) 555-0880
Bedtime: 7:30
Games: Mouse Trap, Uno, kick ball
Books: Mike Mulligan and the Steam Shovel, Amazing Reptiles

GOOD CENTS

Special Touch

Thank You!

50¢ off!

COMMENTS

Thanks!

Show customers how much you appreciate their business.

- **Send thank-you cards.**
- **Give out coupons for 50¢ off the next order or service.**
- **Make follow-up calls to find out if customers are satisfied.**
- **Mail comment cards with bills.**

Keeping Track

Stay **on top** of your **money** with a ledger.

Use red ink for money spent.

Write It Down

Keep a list of the money you've made, the money you've spent, and any other money you've put into your business.

GREEN 🖐 THUMB LEDGER

Date	Description	To/From	Money Spent
3/15	Birthday money	Grandma	
3/21	Allowance	Dad	
4/1	Seeds, peat pots, soil	Garden Central	$15.00
4/21	2 hours weeding	Anne Hamilton	
4/26	2 hours weeding	Mr. Lohr	
4/30	Movies		$10.00
5/1	7 seedlings, 1 hour planting	Anne Hamilton	
5/5	20 herb seedlings	Farmer's Market	

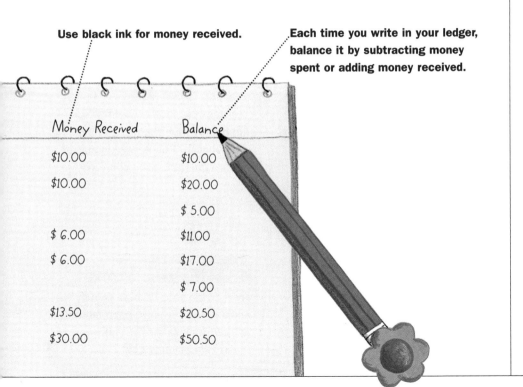

Use black ink for money received.

Each time you write in your ledger, balance it by subtracting money spent or adding money received.

Money Received	Balance
$10.00	$10.00
$10.00	$20.00
	$ 5.00
$ 6.00	$11.00
$ 6.00	$17.00
	$ 7.00
$13.50	$20.50
$30.00	$50.50

GOOD CENTS

Moneymaker Report Card

Measure your success with a moneymaker report card. Add up the money you made and subtract the cost of materials, start-up, advertising, and office supplies. What's left is your profit—money you can spend or save. If you aren't earning enough to make up for your time, think about raising your prices or buying materials in bulk or at a discount store.

$55.50 money made
-25.00 money spent
$30.50 profit :)

Set a Goal

Follow these **steps** to find out how long it will take to reach your **savings goal.**

1. Savings Goal

Write down your savings goal—the total amount you want to save.

2. Spending Money

Before you decide how much money you can save each month, add up how much money you spend each month.

New bike: $100.00

$10.00 Food, clothing, & gifts
+ $ 5.00 Books, magazines, movies
$15.00 Total spending money

$30.50 Profit
-$15.00 Spending money
$ 15.50 Savings each month

$100.00 ÷ $15.50 = 6½ months

3. In the Bank

Subtract the total amount of spending money from the money made each month. This is the amount of money you can save each month.

4. It Takes Time

Then divide your savings goal by the amount you can save each month to find out how long it will take you to reach your savings goal.

Speed It Up

Do you want to reach your savings goal sooner? Maybe you could do without your weekly trip to the ice cream shop or the movies. Think about how you can cut back on spending and increase your savings.

Save It for Later

Here's how **savings-smart** girls squirrel their money away.

I have three plastic containers that I put my money in: one for spending, one for gifts, and one for saving for big things I want to buy myself.

Ali
Massachusetts

I started saving money for a horse six years ago. Now I have more than $500! It's been hard sometimes to keep from spending it, but I just think of how wonderful it will be when I have a horse of my very own!

Elizabeth :-)
Missouri
via e-mail

I save all my change. I put it in a big piggy bank. When it's filled, I take it to the bank to cash it in for dollars. Then I save half of that.

Katie
Wisconsin

Grow Your Money

Opening a savings account is like putting your money in a piggy bank, but it's better because it allows your savings to grow with *interest*. Interest is the money that the bank gives you for the privilege of being able to use your money while it's in the bank. When you're ready to open an account, call the bank to find out what you need to bring and ask a parent or guardian to go with you. You'll receive an account number, a passbook or register to keep track of your money, and deposit and withdrawal slips to put money into and take money out of the account.

OPEN A NEW ACCOUNT TODAY

GOOD CENTS

Stock Up

Are you saving for college or other long-term goals? There are many ways to save for the future. Ask your parents about stocks, bonds, CDs, and other ways to make your money grow even faster.

STOCK MARKET

Shop Smart

You've **worked hard** for your money. Make the most of it by **spending it wisely.**

Spending Limit

Before going shopping, look over how much money you have and how much money you need in the next month or so. Is there any to spare? Decide how much you can spend and leave the rest at home so you won't be tempted to splurge.

Stretch Your Dollar

Spending money carefully doesn't mean you're stingy—it just shows you're clever. Try these tips for stretching your dollars.

1 Buy used books and CDs instead of new ones.

2 Plan ahead and shop around for the best price.

3 Head for the clearance rack in department stores and keep your eye out for sales.

4 Make gifts instead of buying them. Handmade presents are often appreciated more because they show your time, care, and thoughtfulness.

Gotta Have It?

Ever see something in a store that you gotta have? How about those rainbow suspenders you wore only once? Prevent the "wish-I-hadn'ts" by asking yourself these questions:

- Will I use it or wear it often?
- Will I use it or wear it a couple of months from now?
- If I get it, will I have any money left over for what I'm saving for?

If the answer to any of these questions is no, you might want to think twice. If you still aren't sure, try waiting a week to see if it has the same appeal.

Giving Back

Do you want to help save animals or feed the hungry? **Donate** some of your earnings to a charity or raise money for a **good cause.**

Fun-Raiser

Throw a fun-raiser, like a "Hula-thon for Hunger" or a pet show to benefit the local animal shelter, and donate the profits to charity. To choose a cause you want to support, ask parents, teachers, or neighbors which organizations they trust. Find out how the group will use your donation. Then give with pride knowing that you are using your "good cents" to help others!

ANIMAL SHELTER

Tools You Can Use!

Put your **"good cents"** to work with these super business tools. They're removable so you can copy and use them again and again.

Add your personal information and spread the word about your money-maker with business cards.

Make and deliver perfect products by using an order form.

Grab your customers' attention with doorknob flyers.

Write up a bill to let customers know how much they owe, or offer a receipt to show that they've paid.

Label your crafts and goodies with eye-catching price tags.

Let others know you mean business with an open-and-closed sign.

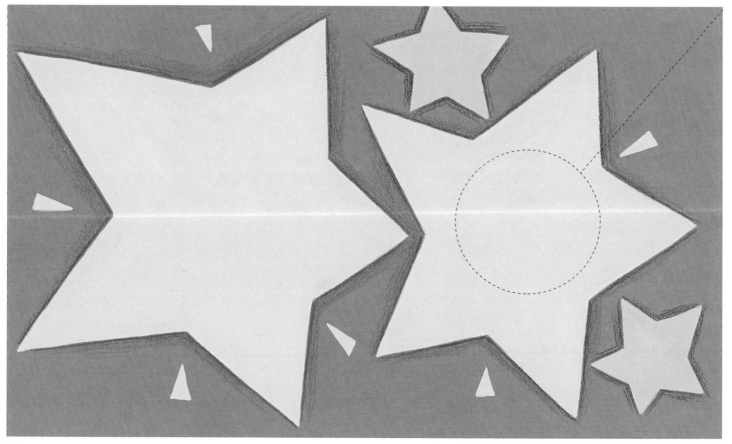

PRICE TAGS

ORDER FORM

Order Form

Date ....

Bill to ....

Delivery date ....

Description

Quantity

Price

Total _____

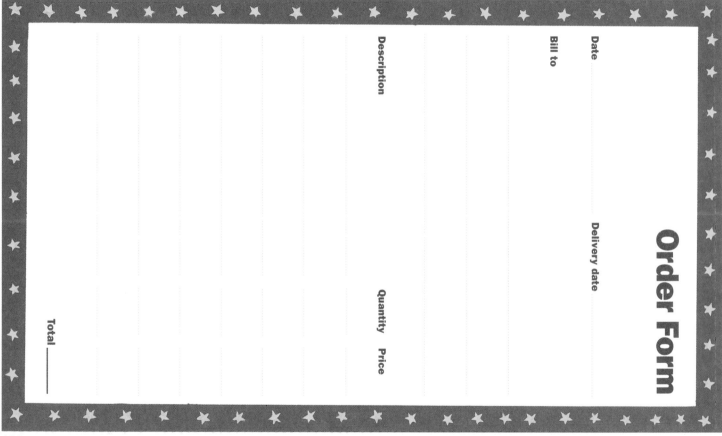

Order Form

Date

Bill to

Delivery date

Description

Quantity   Price

Total ___

Bill

Date

To

Description   **Price**

Please pay by   **Total**

Thank You!

BILL & RECEIPT

Bill

Date

To

Description   **Price**

Please pay by   **Total**_____

Thank You!